Ultimate Guide To Greenhouse Gardening for Beginners

BY LINDSEY PYLARINOS

How to Grow Flowers and Vegetables Year-Round In Your Greenhouse

2nd Edition

Greenhouse Gardening for Beginners 2nd Edition

Copyright 2014 by Lindsey Pylarinos - All rights reserved.

In no way is it legal to reproduce, duplicate, or transmit any part of this document in either electronic means or in printed format. Recording of this publication is strictly prohibited and any storage of this document is not allowed unless with written permission from the publisher. All rights reserved

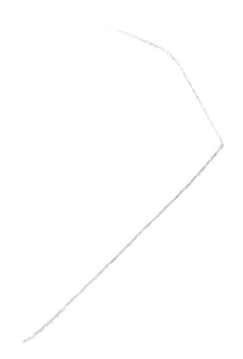

Table of Contents

Introduction 5

Chapter 1: A Short History of the Greenhouse 6

Chapter 2: Why Grow Plants in a Greenhouse? 9

Chapter 3: How to Build Your Greenhouse 13

Chapter 4: Types and Styles of Greenhouse Structures 17

Chapter 5: Types of Greenhouse According to use 22

Chapter 6: Considerations for Greenhouses 25

Chapter 7: Greenhouse Coverings and Frames 28

Chapter 8: Accessories for Greenhouses 32

Chapter 9: Preparing for Growing Season 34

Chapter 10: Planting in Cold Weather 37

Chapter 11: Planting in Warm Weather 39

Chapter 12: Managing the Greenhouse Environment 41

Chapter 13: Growing Vegetables in Greenhouses .. 46

Chapter 14: Growing Fruits in Greenhouses 49

Chapter 15: Growing Herbs in Greenhouses 52

Chapter 16: Growing Ornamental Plants in a Greenhouse 53

Conclusion 56

Check Out My Other Books 57

Introduction

I want to thank you and congratulate you for purchasing the book, *"Greenhouse Gardening for Beginners: How to Grow Flowers and Vegetables Year-Round In Your Greenhouse"*.

This book contains proven steps and strategies on how to start greenhouse gardening from the ground up.

Greenhouse Gardening for Beginners is a comprehensive guide to growing plants inside a greenhouse. From building your greenhouse to raising the right plants at the right times of the year, this book will teach you all you need to know on how to do indoor gardening right.

Thanks again for purchasing this book. I hope you enjoy it!

Chapter 1: A Short History of the Greenhouse

Having your own garden at your backyard is one of the traditional pastimes around the world. Not only does gardening carry its own unique challenges, but it can also be extremely fulfilling if you can get it right. Of course, there is the unique fulfillment of being able to grow plants in your yard. Also, the tangible benefits of growing these plants are there (ex.: food, ornamentals, extra fresh air, etc.). While there are many factors that can dictate the feasibility of backyard gardening, the biggest one of them all is weather.

Extreme weather conditions are considered to be the biggest enemy of anyone engaged in gardening and farming activities. Bad weather can dramatically slow down the growth of plants, reducing their overall productivity in the process. In some cases, extreme weather conditions (heavy rains, drought, high heat, frost) can cause the outright death of plants. Not only does bad weather put a monkey wrench on one's planting activities, but it can potentially cost a planter a ton of money and time due to damage.

One of the best solutions developed to protect plants from the ravages of extreme weather is the greenhouse. It is a building specially designed to facilitate the growing of plants indoors. The sizes of these structures can range from small sheds to large industry-spec buildings. These buildings are made not just to give shelter to plants from extreme weather, but it can also serve as a device to create optimal conditions needed to grow plants.

One of the most enduring characteristics of a greenhouse is its ability to maintain a particular temperature in spite of outside weather conditions. Thanks to its unique design, the interior of a greenhouse can remain warm even if the weather outside is cold (especially during the wintertime). This is made possible because the unique design of the greenhouse (mainly featuring glass, plastic, or other translucent material) absorbs available heat from the sun, heating up air from the inside. At the same time, the greenhouse is made in such a way that warmed air does not get out. While they use the same name, the process that heats up greenhouses is not the same as the greenhouse effect.

While the use of greenhouses is increasing over the last few years (in fact, some of the greenhouses today can be considered as technological marvels), the concept of it has actually existed even during the early days of civilization. The first trace of the greenhouse is seen during the time of the Roman Empire. The gardeners of then-emperor Tiberus developed a planting method that's similar to the greenhouse system to ensure the emperor can get his daily fix of his favorite cucumbers. Greenhouses as we know it today emerged in the 13th century in Italy. They were then created to house exotic plants. The concept of an active greenhouse (a greenhouse with a mechanism that allows for the manual adjustment of temperature) was first developed in Korea during the 15th century.

The golden age for the use of greenhouses was during the Victorian Era. During this time period, it was considered to be a status symbol to have a greenhouse in a home. Another factor that facilitated the rise of interest for greenhouses is the increasing popularity of indoor gardening, indoor farming, and botany. Another cause for the boom in greenhouse building is the continuing improvement of building materials. Not only do these materials made the greenhouses of today more efficient, but it also has somewhat reduced the cost of building them.

Greenhouse Gardening for Beginners 2nd Edition

Nowadays, greenhouses can be found in all shapes, sizes, and styles. There are backyard greenhouses that are constructed using simple materials, and then there are industrial greenhouses with state-of-the-art features that allow farmers to control just about every parameter involved in growing plants. With an increased emphasis on increasing plant productivity and the increasing costs of acquiring land, more people are resorting to greenhouse gardening. The next chapter will focus on the advantages of growing plants in a greenhouse.

Chapter 2: Why Grow Plants in a Greenhouse?

Now that you know the origins of the greenhouse, how it works, and how it has been used by people from different generations, the next question that must be answered is why you should actually use one. Why investing in the construction of a greenhouse is considered a good investment to make as a gardener? Last but not least, what are the advantages, if any, that you can get from growing plants in your own greenhouse? Here are some of the most compelling reasons why you should build your own greenhouse today.

1. A greenhouse allows you to plant all year round- This is the most compelling reason why gardening enthusiasts make use of greenhouses. Whether you are a breeder, a farmer, or a hobbyist, you'll love to have the chance to enjoy gardening 24/7. Unfortunately, the fact is that you can't do exactly that on a lot of places in the world. A greenhouse provides you with the opportunity to grow your plants indoors while weather conditions outside are less than ideal. With the ability to change up conditions inside the greenhouse, you can grow particular plants there in any part of the year.

2. Indoor gardening allows for better breeding control- Breeding can be such a tricky thing in itself. External factors can have a huge impact on how a specific plant differentiates itself from one generation to the next. While these external factors can prove very advantageous breeding-wise in the wild, there is also a higher probability that you won't get the characteristics you desire from your plant if you choose to breed outdoors. By taking your breeding projects at the greenhouse, you can virtually shut off potential factors that can meddle with your breeding process. This way, you

increase your odds of getting exactly the characteristics that you want from your plants.

3. It allows you to control environmental conditions- For most gardening enthusiasts, this is the biggest reason why they go for greenhouses to begin with. On the great outdoors, it's virtually up to your plants to take whatever Mother Nature has to dish out. In terms of survival odds, that is not exactly the most ideal scenario. This is where the greenhouse comes into the picture. You can control some of the most basic environmental parameters such as temperature, soil moisture, light exposure, and humidity inside the greenhouse. Some modern forms of these buildings provide the gardener total control of all external factors that affect plant growth.

4. A greenhouse protects your plants from destructive elements- This is another element that makes greenhouse gardening stand out. There are so many things that can go wrong in gardening and it goes beyond the state of the weather. The presence of pests, animals, weeds, and parasites can all knock down your plants. Not only do these take away from the potential benefits you can reap from these plants, but they can also put their lives in considerable danger. Inside the shelter of a greenhouse, you can prevent these organisms from touching your plants. Other than for damage control, this is also great as a means for reducing your dependence on potentially harmful products such as pesticides.

5. It allows you to grow different kinds of plants- There is power in variety when it comes to gardening. If you can grow different kinds of plants in your backyard, that is a distinct advantage. You can do exactly that with the help of a greenhouse. When growing plants outdoors, what you can plant and when you can plant them is entirely dependent on

where you live and what the season is. With the help of your greenhouse, you can create an environment that suits the needs of specific plants you otherwise can't grow outside or in a particular time of the year. This makes gardening more fun and more interesting.

6. A greenhouse adds style to your home- Remember that 2 centuries ago, a greenhouse is considered to be a sign of wealth? More than for just being a status symbol, having a greenhouse is surely attractive. When properly organized, the greenhouse in itself can be a wonderful structure. It's also a great way to add some greens into your home. It's like having a real garden, only you're maintaining it indoors! While most people who build a greenhouse don't really think much about style points, you do get it for your home when you get it right.

7. It can potentially add to your bottom line- Perhaps you already know how having your own garden has its own earning potential. Did you know that with the help of a greenhouse, you can potentially expand your bottom line as a gardener? All of this is made possible by the various strategic advantages provided by greenhouses. You can raise plants at virtually any time of the year, you can optimize various conditions so your plants may thrive, you can prevent external factors from compromising the health and qualities of your plants, and you can raise plants that would otherwise not grow well outdoors. All those factors send your garden's productivity (and ultimately its potential profitability) sky-high. Having a greenhouse is great for business to say the least.

Having a greenhouse can prove helpful for gardeners of all levels. Whether you are a hobbyist, a businessman, a researcher, or someone who just loves the idea of raising plants in their own backyard, you can enjoy the benefits of the greenhouse. Build yours today and see the difference.

Chapter 3: How to Build Your Greenhouse

Perhaps by now you already know why having your own greenhouse makes a lot of sense. You can get so many benefits from having a greenhouse right at your own backyard. Of course, to get engaged with greenhouse gardening, you'll need to have a greenhouse ready! This is where construction comes into the picture. This chapter will serve as your guide to building your greenhouse from the ground up.

1. Plan first where you'll place your greenhouse- Location is everything when it comes to any construction project. Building your own greenhouse, whether you are putting it up for hobby or business purposes, requires some pre-planning to ensure that you'll get the most out of it. The first thing you must consider is the size of the building. How much space can you realistically allot for your greenhouse? Another thing you must consider is the direction where your greenhouse would be facing. As a rule of thumb, it's recommended that the building should face the east so it would receive the most morning sun.

2. Prep the construction area- After planning where you'll put up your greenhouse, the next thing you must do is to prep the area where it shall eventually stand. In this step, you must ensure that you cover all the building essentials. One thing you must cover is drainage, especially if you live in an area where rains occur regularly. It is encouraged that the ground must be filled if it shows signs of being uneven. At the same time, your greenhouse must have access to electricity. It must be part of the construction plan to create a system that directs electricity to the greenhouse.

Greenhouse Gardening for Beginners 2nd Edition

3. Set up your greenhouse for sun reception- This step is of special importance if you are planning to grow plants well into the winter season. One reason why it's recommended that the greenhouse must face east is because it has a higher chance to receive optimal amounts of sunlight regardless of season. For reference, sunlight during the winter is more angled than during the summer, where light rays are more or less traveling straight down. Make sure that there's little or no interference coming from trees, buildings, and other tall structures as they can make sunlight reception more difficult.

4. Decide which route you'll take for building your greenhouse- There are 2 main ways to build your greenhouse: creating one from scratch or making use of kits. The main advantage of creating a greenhouse from scratch is that it allows you to build a greenhouse that's tailor-made for your personal preferences. On the other hand, building a greenhouse thru a kit would make the building process simpler and more precise. If you don't have prior building experience, a kit is better suited for you. If you want maximum control on which features go into your greenhouse, then designing one from scratch is the route to go. Just remember that you got to make precise measurements either way to ensure your building won't either be too big or too small for your plan.

5. Check your building materials- Going for a building kit or getting materials from scratch will both cost money. On the average, creating a greenhouse for home use would cost you anywhere between 500 and 5000 dollars. Because of this, you got to see to it that the materials you'll use would be of the best quality possible. When trying to purchase a kit, make sure to perform prior inspection and also check reviews about the product. All the parts, especially those that

would constitute the frame, must be sturdy enough to last for years.

6. Choose which building style you want- There are 3 main ways to build your greenhouse, with each style carrying its own unique advantages. A lean-to design makes use of a pre-existing wall from an adjacent building, meaning you'll get more support while using fewer materials. Rebars, beams, and supports are often sufficient enough to create a lean-on greenhouse. A Quonset frame features a domed ceiling that can be made using a combination of steel and PVC. It can be built using fewer materials, and the domed shape can prove to be more receptive to receiving sunlight. A rigid frame is remarkable for its superior durability and design. While such a design can prove costly in terms of both materials and manpower, it is the best long-term option for avid gardeners.

7. Choose covering material- Once you have chosen your framework, it is now time to choose which material to use to cover your frame. A greenhouse can be covered using different materials, with each option having their own unique set of advantages. Plastic film such as polyethylene is remarkably inexpensive. While it doesn't hold heat as good as most covering materials, its low-maintenance nature is great for recreational growers. Using double-walled plastic provides better energy efficiency and sun absorption, though it costs slightly more than using plastic film. Using fiberglass, most especially high-grade fiberglass, would give you the best compromise between using glass and plastic, thanks to its combination of conductivity, durability, and low cost. Glass, while expensive, provides the best characteristics needed to maintain a hardcore greenhouse.

8. Build from the ground up- Now that you have a plan in place, it is now time to ensure that everything would be as stable as planned. It would all start with the framework.

Adding stakes and reinforcements would help ensure that the structure would remain stable. Aside from adding reinforcement, keeping the ground stable would also help a lot. Other than keeping the framework stable, there are other ways to make your structure more durable. Treating wood would help in strengthening it. When placing your covering material of your choice, it is important that you seal it to the frame as close as you can.

9. Install auxiliary accessories- Depending on how you intend to build your greenhouse for, you can install some external accessories that help maintain the optimal condition for your plants. One important environmental factor that must be controlled is temperature. You can control ambient temperature in your greenhouse by installing accessories such as vents, fans, and even thermostats. You can also add lights so that your plants can receive adequate lighting even during low-light seasons. With some accessories for greenhouses becoming more sophisticated, they give more power and flexibility for the greenhouse grower.

10. Have a water source in place- Any kind of plant needs water for it to thrive. Because of this, you got to put in place a watering system for your greenhouse. When installing a watering system, you can either go for a simple structure or a complex one. It all depends on your budget. Regardless, one thing you must sort out is the piping system. Ideally, your greenhouse must have a stand-alone piping system that distributes water at every corner of the greenhouse. This would make watering a much easier task, especially if you're intending to have a large structure in place. You can then install watering aids such as sprinklers, hoses, and cisterns once you've established your water supply.

Chapter 4: Types and Styles of Greenhouse Structures

One major decision in building a greenhouse is choosing the method of putting together your own greenhouse, which includes the type and style of the structures. It's already been previously discussed what the advantages and disadvantages are of erecting your own greenhouse from scratch and building one from a pre-planned kit. The general building styles of greenhouses were also described. This chapter will delve deeper and explain the types of greenhouse structures, the different greenhouse styles, and the different purposes that they serve.

The first greenhouse building structure that we will discuss is the lean-to design. Since this particular design shares a wall with a pre-existing edifice, the most obvious advantage is a lower construction cost. These lean-to designs are ideal if you don't have a lot of space and they're also closer to water, heat and electricity. The typical material for this is glass, and the ideal location for this type of greenhouse should be to the side of a home with a southern exposure. A common disadvantage for this type of greenhouse is that temperature control can be more challenging due to the fact that the wall that the greenhouse is built on may collect the sun's heat, while the wall windows of the greenhouse may swiftly lose heat.

The next greenhouse type is called even span. Even span greenhouses are single houses that have roofs with an even width and even pitch. It is usually attached to a house with a gable end. This has greater design flexibility, and its framework is usually made from steel, wood or aluminum. Its covering is usually made of permanent or semipermanent material like glass or structured sheets. Since it has greater exposed glass area, it uses up more heat, which mean it costs more than the lean-to design.

The ridge and furrow greenhouses are comprised of several even-span greenhouses that are attached to one another, connecting a row of greenhouses. There are no shared walls to maximize growing space. Instead, the houses are connected by gutters which help transport water, usually from the north to south direction. The Venlo is a modification of the ridge and furrow structure. In Venlo, the gable ends are very narrow which allows for the use of narrow bars and single panes of glass to be used on the roof. This is done so that a higher amount of light will reach the crop.

The hoop house is a greenhouse type that evolved from the even span structure. They are usually constructed using bent tubular PVC pipes which act as the framework, which are then covered with a single layer of plastic. Sometimes, a second layer is added for extra insulation. Hoop houses are inexpensive alternatives to even span greenhouses, although the plastic covering may need to be replaced every 4 years or so. This is easy to build, though not as sturdy as other greenhouse structures.

Another type of greenhouse is the window-mounted structure. This is ideal for those growers that have no extra land space available, especially those who live in apartment buildings or condominiums. These are great for growing vegetables, herbs and small plants. The structure usually juts off the exterior wall of the house, which allows for the maximum penetration of light. It typically also has windows that can open on both sides, which allows utmost air ventilation. The window mount is made of glass and is available in a variety of sizes, either in single units or in tandem arrangements for larger windows. This is available in pre-fabricated forms, and should be attached to the side of the house facing a southern exposure.

One sub-type of window mount is called the window farm. It is a vertical, indoor garden which uses natural window light and organic liquid soil, or hydroponic system. Growers prefer this if they want to grow their own fresh vegetables even if they don't have a backyard. However, hydroponic farming needs more materials such as pumps, tubes and fertilizers and requires more maintenance than the usual greenhouse.

Another greenhouse structure gaining popularity today especially for those with limited space is the cold frame. This is the simplest and cheapest greenhouse structure. This is simply a small greenhouse with an open bottom, and it can be covered with almost anything, from glass to plastic sheeting. The only consideration is that the covering should allow for heat ventilation. For some growers, it just provides a supplemental greenhouse to extend the growing season. Traditionally, it's been used as an addition to the heated greenhouse. Its main drawback is it could cause overheating of plants, and since the materials are not as sturdy, they are prone to damage or breakage.

The last type of structure that we will discuss is the free standing greenhouse, which is a separate structure that has side walls, end walls and a roof. Unlike the even span structure, free-standing is set apart from other buildings in the house to maximize sunlight.

Free-standing greenhouses have five fundamental styles. These are the gothic arch, Quonset, rigid frame, A-frame and post and rafter.

Greenhouse Gardening for Beginners 2nd Edition

A Gothic arch or a Quonset greenhouse is one of the most well-known styles of greenhouses. It is comprised of a semi-circular frame which is built from galvanized pipe. The frame is usually round or semi-circular, and covered with plastic sheeting, which is easily expandable. Named after the World War II military barracks, Quonset greenhouses have a simple and efficient design, which allows the greatest amount of sunlight out of all greenhouse designs. However, storage space and headroom is lost because of the domed roof. The Gothic arch is similar to Quonset, but it is taller. This provides more wall space and headroom. The freestanding architecture of a Quonset or Gothic arch design is ideal in an open field or backyard facing the north-south orientation.

Another style is the rigid frame, which is a traditional style building with more air and interior space. The rigid frame design has vertical sidewalls and rafters. There are no columns to support the roof. Instead, nailed plywood connects the sidewall supports to the rafters to create one rigid frame. This style needs a good foundation in order to support the lateral load on the sidewalls.

The A-frame design is common, and it is simple and requires fewer materials than the conventional design, which is inherently similar. The structure is composed of combining the roof and side walls to create a triangular building. The usual materials used for A-frame are glass or fiberglass. Pre-fabricated materials also use rigid translucent polycarbonate glazing panels, which has a lower cost compared to both glass and fiberglass. The disadvantage of using this style is that the narrow side walls limit the use of the entire area, and air circulation can be a challenge in the corners. The ideal location for the A-frame design is in a south-facing open field or backyard.

Greenhouse Gardening for Beginners 2nd Edition

Another common free-standing design is the Post and Rafter greenhouse, or conventional type. This is a traditional building with a roofing framework that supports heavy glass and fiberglass. This design has the maximum amount of space and has one of the strongest rafters that lend support to the roof. Since this design requires more materials, the cost is higher compared to other design options.

The type of greenhouse structure and style that you choose will solely depend on your budget, the available space, your preferences and your goals for building a greenhouse.

Chapter 5: Types of Greenhouse According to use

Greenhouses can be used to grow different types of plants. Since greenhouse environments can be adjusted and altered based on the plants that you want to grow, it is best to decide what your purpose is for having a greenhouse before building one. Your greenhouse can be used to grow vegetables or fruits, orchids or ornamental plants. Each type of plant requires a different type of environment. While it is possible to take care of all various kinds of plants inside one greenhouse, it will prove to be a challenging task to simulate different types of environments to make all these plants flourish. It is best to put together plants that will more or less flourish in the same type of environment in one greenhouse.

This chapter will discuss specific types of greenhouses designed for specific uses or purposes.

The first type of greenhouse according to use is a tropical greenhouse. This type requires a lot of money to heat, especially in a place where one gets cold weather. In order to heat the greenhouse in a level required by tropical plants, triple glass panes or additional greenhouse glazing is needed. During winter, temperature inside the greenhouse must be between 50 to 65 degrees Fahrenheit at night and 75 degrees to 80 degrees Fahrenheit during the day time. The reason behind this is although tropical plants need a warm environment, they do not need to be placed under direct sunlight. They need humidity, so greenhouse materials have to withstand this type of environment. To prevent a greenhouse from overheating, large vents or blower fans must be used to circulate moist, hot air.

When you have decided to build a tropical greenhouse, you would need a good quality heater with thermostat, power supply; waterproof lights with timers to extend the day length of plants, fans, automatic vent opening system and misting and watering system and low-temperature alarms.

The next type of greenhouse according to use is the orchid greenhouse. There are some growers who just want to grow orchids and nothing else, so they need to have a greenhouse with an environment that is conducive to orchid growth. Orchids have specific temperature and light needs. They require no more than 30 degrees of temperature shift from day to night. We have a separate discussion in growing orchids in a greenhouse in succeeding chapters, but generally, orchids thrive in different and very specific daytime and night time conditions as well. You still need to decide what types of orchids you want to propagate.

Generally however, most orchids do not grow in an environment that has a lot of exhaust fumes from heaters and pesticides.

Orchid greenhouses need a good quality electric heater, misting or humidifying systems, waterproof lights, power supply, fans, vent opening system, thermometers and humidity gauges, low-temperature alarms, and a watering system.

An alpine greenhouse requires conditions that re-create high altitudes where plants are covered with frozen snow or ice. A greenhouse that replicates the needs of alpine plants should prepare for blooming in the short summer months. Plants in this greenhouse environment should be very cold but protected from snow or water. Alpine houses often have windows that allow air to circulate but do not allow rain and snow inside. Ample ventilation is needed by alpine plants and the humidity in the air should be kept as low as possible.

Greenhouse Gardening for Beginners 2nd Edition

In temperate countries, an alpine greenhouse is an advantage because heating is not required anymore, so costs for the upkeep of the greenhouse will go down.

Chapter 6: Considerations for Greenhouses

If you have already decided on the type of greenhouse structure, style and use that is suitable to you, then it is also essential to know certain factors and considerations in either buying pre-fabricated greenhouses or building your own. The considerations are heating, ventilation, humidity, panel clarity and flexibility.

Heating is crucial for a greenhouse, and the ideal temperature inside should be from 80 to 85 degrees Fahrenheit. The internal temperature must be kept steady. Interior heat mainly comes from the sun, but there are other supplemental heat sources which will be discussed in the next few chapters. On a warm, sunny day, the internal temperature could easily go up to 100 degrees Fahrenheit, and that could easily kill the plants. Therefore, regulating the temperature is extremely important. Proper insulation also affects the heat inside the greenhouse. The prevailing weather in your area will tell you the amount of insulation that's needed for your greenhouse. The main goal is the covering should hold heat within, naturally keeping it warm once cold weather hits and should also allow you to heat your greenhouse in a cost-effective way.

Ventilation or airflow is another important thing to consider in building or buying greenhouses. All greenhouses must include vents. It could either be a top vent that opens a hatch in the ceiling or side vents that bring hot air out and bring in cooler air. You should look for sufficient allowance for air to enter and exit the greenhouse structure. Vents could either operate manually or automatically, depending on your budget. Vent systems would be discussed in greater detail in the next few chapters. To ensure good ventilation, it is a good idea to open the door on warm days and as needed, you may use additional stand fans to keep the air moving.

Controlling the humidity is another consideration. The greenhouse needs humidity, at least 50% or higher. To add humidity in the air, growers place trays of pebbles covered in water underneath the plants. As the water evaporates, it will add humidity.

Panel clarity also creates a huge difference in greenhouses. There are some greenhouses with clear coverings or panels, while there are also some that have opaque or translucent coverings. Currently, there are also semi-diffused models being sold in the market. Clear coverings dispense direct light, while opaque or translucent models give diffused light. It really depends on the purpose and use of the greenhouse. For greenhouses that germinate seeds and grow starters which will eventually be transplanted outdoors, then a clear covering will be able to bring in full, direct sunlight needed by the starter trays. This is because it will encourage the germinating seeds to sprout and develop. If the use of the greenhouse is to develop the plant to maturity, then a translucent or opaque covering will be able to bring in balanced light for even foliage growth. It is highly recommended that one use diffused light in their greenhouses because the plants will develop better. After all, the light that produces the best photosynthesis are actually less bright than direct light and invisible to the human eye.

If you want to get the best of both worlds, semi-diffused covers give the benefits of both clear and opaque or translucent covers. The semi-diffused covers make the greenhouse effective for many different purposes.

Lastly, the flexibility of the greenhouse should be considered. The structure and style should allow for certain customized work according to your needs. You should be able to arrange the shelving in accordance to the gardening plan. Shallow shelves are used for germinating seeds and for starter plants, while taller shelves are for mature plants. There are also greenhouses designed to accommodate additional space for growing more plants.

After all of these things are considered, then it is time to move on to the next crucial decision, which is deciding what type of covering material and framework should be used for the greenhouse.

Chapter 7: Greenhouse Coverings and Frames

Once the type and style of the greenhouse structure has been decided on, and the points for consideration are already addressed, another crucial decision has to be made - the type of covering material and framework that will be used for your greenhouse. There are a lot of options to choose from, each with their own pros and cons.

Greenhouse coverings or glazing, have varying degrees of insulation based on their properties. Foundations, walls and roofs can be insulated and covered.

There are different types of covering materials available in the market today, and they usually come in sheets or panels. Clear plastic and glass work the same way. They both let light to through while keeping the heat inside. They do have their pros and cons though. Plastics are typically not as expensive as glass and lighter in weight, but they are not as durable, especially when exposed to weather. Glass greenhouses may require a bit more to build, but they are more durable.

Here are some types of greenhouse coverings:

1. Fiberglass. This material is translucent, so it gives well-diffused light. It retains heat more efficiently compared to glass. Depending on exposure to the sun, its outer surface becomes brittle and yellowed after 6 to 10 years of use. It also burns easily after a few years, so its insulation and light transmission is greatly reduced. The use of fiberglass has significantly declined due to

the rise of newer materials such as polycarbonates and acrylics.

2. Polyethylene. UV-treated polyethylene film is used to cover huge greenhouses because it costs cheaper than glass and it is easier to maintain. Majority of greenhouses built today is covered in polyethylene. The light transmission of polyethylene is similar to glass, as it provided semi-diffused light, although it is more inexpensive. However, the plastic film has to be replaced every 3-5 years due to the effects of UV light. It also has the tendency to sag and stretch in windy or snowy conditions. Another disadvantage is that it could have high humidity levels.

There are double-covered polyethylene greenhouses. Also called twin-wall polyethylene, these high-density sheets are more rigid than the single film. The double cover provides good insulation. It provides diffused light without letting 75% of natural light to go through.

3. Polycarbonates. Polycarbonates are durable, lightweight and have a long lifespan of 15 years or longer. Although they provide the same clarity as glass, they are not as scratch resistant compared to tempered glass. Multiple-walled polycarbonates have internal air space that gives added strength and insulation, which considerably bring down heating costs. They provide diffused light penetration and can withstand snow and freezing weather, hail and fire. Since they are quite flexible, they can be bent around hoop structures. However, this material can be more expensive than glass.

4. Acrylic. Acrylic sheets give the same insulation value as polycarbonates. They offer better light transmission,

and they last to 10 years. However, it is less flexible than polycarbonates and is more prone to damage.

5. Glass. Glass is an excellent covering because it does not degrade in the sunlight, and reflects heat radiated from within the glasshouse.

6. Tempered glass. Tempered glass is stronger and more durable than regular glass. They are impact-resistant and withstand seasonal changes in temperature. It is more expensive than polycarbonate panels. However, they are more durable and scratch-resistant. Since it is clear, it provides no diffusion.

Like greenhouse glazing, frames are also available in a variety of materials. Choosing the right one depends on your budget and glasshouse needs.

1. Wood. Wood is often used for do-it-yourself greenhouse projects. It provides sufficient durability and strength. However, wood is susceptible to rot, especially if it comes in contact with moisture.

2. Aluminum. Aluminum is strong and lightweight, and it also does not rust. It also has a very long life span.

3. Plastic resin. Plastic resin is cheaper than aluminum and does not conduct heat out of the greenhouse compared to metal frames. Since they lack the strength of metal frames, they are suitable only for smaller greenhouses. They are usually designed to be paired with polycarbonate panels.

4. Steel. Galvanized steel frames are long lasting and have low cost. Because the material is ultra-strong by nature, minimal structure is required when framing. Polyethylene film is typically paired with steel frames.

Greenhouse Gardening for Beginners 2nd Edition

This type of frame is very sturdy, and is usually used for commercial greenhouses.

Chapter 8: Accessories for Greenhouses

Now that the glazing, frames and structure for the greenhouse are in place, it could already be built. When the greenhouse is erected, it is time to think about what accessories should be included in order to make gardening easier. There are some necessary accessories that should be part of the greenhouse. We can always add more as the need arises or the budget allows.

Greenhouse shade cloths are accessories that are useful if you have a semi-diffused or clear greenhouse. It can be draped over the roof to lower the temperature inside. Shade cloths can be installed on top of the greenhouse so that it is easy to draw them out as needed.

Greenhouse benches are tables to hold plants off the floor. They usually come in a variety of materials such as wood, metal, aluminum or plastic. Wooden benches have a tray insert to keep moisture away from the wood, while metal benches have a mesh top to drain water. The advantages of using benches are: the crop is at a reachable, convenient height, there's allowance for good water drainage, and there is good air circulation around the plants. Nowadays, many greenhouses have rolling benches. These can be rolled sideways and this allows for flexibility because the benches can be moved around versus standard fixed benches.

Custom shelving is needed to maximize space usage and for you to be able to customize the interior layout of the greenhouse.

Hand-watering wands are used for young sprouts. It delivers the water through misting so that tender sprouts don't get flattened. It also allows you to reach different shelf heights.

Seed staring supplies and trays are also needed in order to begin propagating plants the right way. There are also a variety of growing mediums and plant supports available in the market.

In order to transport pots, flowers, trees and greenhouse equipment easily, carts and wagons should be used. There are many types of transporters available in the market from all-purpose wagons, dump carts for soil and dirt and garden carts.

Chapter 9: Preparing for Growing Season

Once you have successfully put up your greenhouse, it's time to start planting. Simple as that, right? Not so fast. Your job as a planter doesn't end in creating your greenhouse. In fact, it's just getting started. Just like in conventional gardening, you'll need to prep everything to ensure that your plants will grow according to plan. Your greenhouse is ready for the growing season, but is the gardener ready for it? Here is the step-by-step process of preparing your greenhouse for growing season.

1. Take note of the time of the year- Having an innate knowledge of the seasons is an important skill any seasoned gardener has. No matter where you are, particular seasons on the calendar bring about particular weather parameters, and these parameters would ultimately determine which plants would grow best for that season. While there are plants that grow all year round, there are those that best thrive during a particular season. There are some plants that are at their best during spring and summer, and there are others that are at their best during fall and winter. Take into consideration the time of the year and you'll improve your chances of a great harvest.

2. Study about the plant you're intending to cultivate- Gardeners would say that you'll need to get to know your plants. Taking care of a plant is almost like taking care of a person: if you understand its needs, then you'll have a better shot of providing adequate care for them. With that said, it is highly encouraged that you must know your plants. While nothing teaches better than personal experience, even just reading up about a plant would give you info that would prove invaluable as you raise them. From the conditions they need to grow optimally to their growth patterns and

Greenhouse Gardening for Beginners 2nd Edition

behaviors, understanding the characteristics of your plant will prove invaluable in all stages of gardening.

3. Get your planting zones ready- Whether you are planting on the ground or on pots, prepping your soil properly is very important. While some soils and growth mediums are fertile by itself, it's considered a rule of thumb to add fertilizer (it's highly encouraged to go organic if possible) before the start of growing season. This will ensure that it contains enough nutrients to make your plant thrive. Before planting, consider which medium a particular plant grows best. Some thrive on mediums that are sand-like, while others thrive on clay-like surfaces. You also have to monitor other characteristics of your planting medium such as pH, as they can either help or hurt your plant's chances of growing healthy.

4. Sow your seeds well- Planting seeds are not as easy as just dropping them to the ground and observing what happens next. While this approach works in both nature and traditional farming, doing this greatly reduces the chances of your seeds to survive. Just like newborn children need special care after they come out of the womb, your seeds also need special care to ensure they will thrive once they come out. This is where sowing techniques come into the picture. Planting seeds at the right depth and keeping different seeds at safe distance from each other ensures will prove extremely helpful. Once the seeding has emerged, properly planting the seedling gives it a head start as it starts its journey to become a healthy adult plant.

5. Administer timely care for your plants- You got to be there for your plants when they need you. You got to closely monitor each of them to see if there's something wrong so you can resolve it before it gets worse. You must water your plants at specific times of the day while also making sure that

the water you provide is neither too much nor too little. You also got to see to it that no pest comes inside your greenhouse and predate on your plants. You can also adjust specific parameters in your greenhouse whenever necessary, which would be discussed further on the next step.

6. Use your accessories when necessary- Particular devices are included in your design plan for a reason. Also, you installed a long list of accessories in your greenhouse for a reason. If you made the effort and investment to install them, make sure to use them to your advantage! Conditions can either get too hot or too cold. During these situations, you can make use of your various climate control apparatuses. While the most basic climate control devices only have vents, fans, and passive outlets, some go as far as having an automated heating/cooling system for their greenhouse. You can also make use of lights so that your plants can receive enough light even when there's not enough sun outside. The best gardeners use their greenhouse accessories to the hilt.

Chapter 10: Planting in Cold Weather

One of the main reasons why people create greenhouses is because it allows them to plant all year round. To be more specific, they are preparing for the colder months of fall and winter. While having a greenhouse will provide you the opportunity to grow the so-called winter plants effectively, it is no guarantee that you'll be able to raise them well. You'll still need to equip yourself with the right techniques for raising plants in cold weather. Here are some tips that can help you get by, as well as some plants that are best suited for such weather conditions.

Growing cold weather plants during the winter seasons allow you to make very minimal adjustments to the conditions inside your greenhouse. Often times, the minimal amount of sunlight received during these cold periods is more than enough to provide heat sufficient enough for these plants to survive. In fact, subjecting them to summer-type temperatures can prove detrimental for their growth. Another advantage of planting cold weather plants during this season is the fact that they can withstand even occasional freezing temperatures.

There is a huge variety of plants that can be considered at home with cold weather. You can grow these plants on low-temperature, low-light conditions without encountering too much problems. Among the staples of cold weather growing include leafy plants such as cabbage, lettuce, and spinach. Cruciferous vegetables such as broccoli and cauliflower also thrive in such conditions. Also, plants that grow massive roots such as beets and carrots are known to be cold weather plants. Other plants that are known to thrive during this time of the year include peas, radishes, turnips, green onions, chard, and kohlrabi.

A lot of these plants are capable of growing with minimal supervision and without any special treatment. Of course, you got to make sure that you provide your plants with sufficient care at all times. To ensure that your plants would grow accordingly, here are some tips that can prove useful.

1. Avoid temperature extremes- While cold weather plants are resilient to temperature changes, it is not advisable to expose these plants to either extreme cold or heat. Make sure to not make your greenhouse either too hot or too cold. As these plants are more used to cool weather, too much heat would not be conducive for their growth. As a final reminder, it's not healthy for the plant to be subjected to temperature fluctuations as it's a source of stress for them.

2. Keep the light flowing- Getting light is a bit tricky especially during the winter season. As days are shorter during the cold months, you'll need to make the most out of the sunlight that comes in. However, you might need to supplement some light thru your built-in lighting system. This is especially so for seedlings still at the nursery. In fact, some seeds don't sprout without enough light. As a guide, study the photoperiod of the specific plant you're intending to cultivate.

Chapter 11: Planting in Warm Weather

While some people think that the greenhouse is only designed for cool weather planting, it is actually designed to be used for any weather condition. Gardening is fun to do during the months of spring and summer, so why should you hold back from growing your favorite plants? As long as you know the right skills and techniques needed to grow plants during this season, you can enjoy the company of plants that thrive during the warmer times of the year. Here are some tips that can help you grow plants in your greenhouse during warm weather as well as which plants are great to grow during this season.

Usually, you grow plants outdoors during the warm season. However, growing indoors offers more potential for growth than giving some extra hours of sunlight. It saves you from contending with all other factors that may cause problems for you and your plants. This is the time when you'll have to plant warm weather plants. The relatively high temperatures combined with the direct and uninterrupted supply of sunlight will make these plants flourish. They also thrive during nights when temperature is moderately warm.

There are numerous plants that flourish during warm weather. Fruit-bearing plants such as watermelon, melon, squash, and tomatoes all thrive in situations when both light and warmth are at a constant supply. Tropical plants such as citrus plants, peppers, eggplant, and cucumber also grow prominently under these conditions. Other popular plants such as beans and berries also thrive under these conditions. As long as you get to know about the needs of each individual plant, you should not have too much problem raising warm weather plants inside a greenhouse.

Greenhouse Gardening for Beginners 2nd Edition

Planting in warm weather may seem like a walk in the park, but there is absolutely no room for complacency here. Just like in cold weather, things can go wrong even when there's sufficient sunlight around. Here are some tips that can guide you when raising plants in warm weather.

1. Be careful of too much heat and humidity- While these so-called warm weather plants are adept on surviving on warm environments, there is always such a thing as too much warmth. When the weather gets too hot, your plants will literally wilt. In fact, it has been estimated that most garden plants can only tolerate up to 90-100 degrees F at most. When it gets hot, you'll need to make use of temperature management systems such as fans and vents. You can also control the humidity inside your greenhouse.

2. Water your plants wisely- Watering your plants is a crucial element of taking care of plants during the spring and summer. The amount of water needed by a specific plant is generally dependent on its individual needs. Other than making sure that their needs are satisfied, you also got to watch out for creating too much humidity. Because of this, it is generally recommended that you water your plants twice a day: during the middle of noon and during the night.

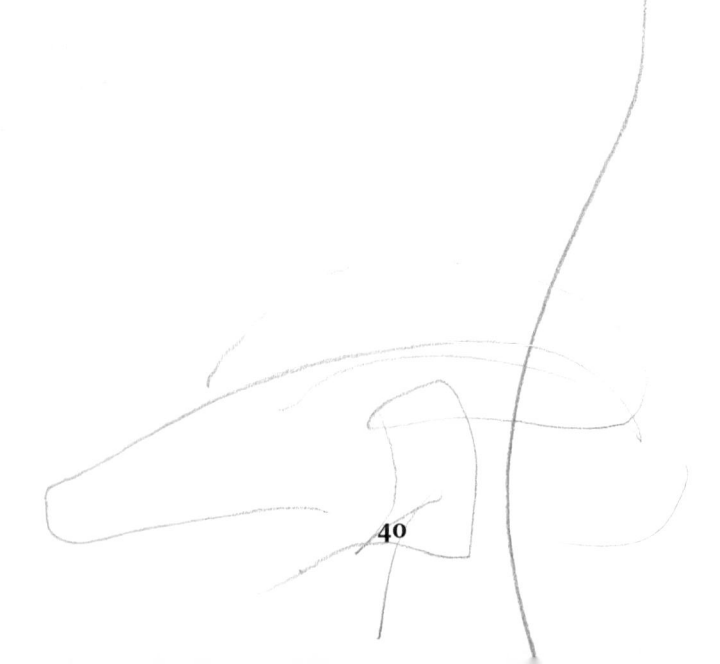

Chapter 12: Managing the Greenhouse Environment

The environmental system inside a greenhouse is important because we need to provide a suitable environment for plants to grow. Regulating the environment involves heating, cooling and ventilation, humidity, lighting and watering systems.

Greenhouse heating systems are used in greenhouses to increase temperature within. Three systems are used. These are hot water, steam, infrared heating and forced hot air. Newer greenhouses use hot water as the source of heat because modern boilers are very efficient and small. A hot water system is comprised of a boiler that heats the water and pumps that move the heated water through pipes strategically placed within the greenhouse. Pipes are usually laid out under greenhouse benches, through walls or buried in the concrete floor. The advantage of a hot water heating system is it requires low maintenance. Another advantage is that heat is delivered evenly and could be adjusted within the greenhouse environment, depending on what growing crops require.

The steam heating system uses large boilers that bring water to the boiling point until it steams. Steam then flows through pipes. Steam boilers require frequent maintenance and the heat is not as evenly distributed compared to hot water system. It is also hard to adjust the temperature.

Infrared heating systems are mounted on top of the greenhouse, and heat energy is reflected directly on the plants below. The floor, soil, and greenhouse benches absorb the heat and transfer it to the plants. The plants are kept at the ideal temperature, but the air within the greenhouse remains cooler.

For those who have smaller greenhouses, they use forced hot air heaters because they are cheaper and easy to use. The heaters are hung inside the greenhouse, and air is heated within the units and blown by fans. Depending on the size of the greenhouse, it may need several units strategically positioned inside so that heated air may be distributed evenly.

Another type of forced hot air heater is the horizontal airflow fan, which moves heated air from one direction down to one side of the greenhouse, then back again in the opposite direction down to the other side. The fans are hung from the ceiling, and the circular air pattern moves heated air efficiently around the greenhouse. Aside from providing heat, the system's heating technology can be turned off so that it can provide much-needed air movement or ventilation during warm days.

Aside from heating, greenhouses also need cooling and ventilation systems for warmer days. The most common form of greenhouse ventilation is through vents. Vents are usually located along the sidewalls and along the ridge of the greenhouse. Modern greenhouses have whole roof sections that can be opened. When the temperature within the greenhouse gets too high, motorized vents are activated and opened, which allows hot air to be expelled.

The fan and pad cooling system involve the use of cellulose pads which are installed on one wall within the greenhouse. The pads are maintained so that it is wet at all times using a system of pumps and gutter than circulate water. On the opposite ends of the pads are fans. They pull the air through the pads across the greenhouse, creating cooler air as air outside passes through the pads.

There are greenhouses that utilize both cooling systems – vents and fan and pad cooling.

During the summer months, air movement using cooling systems may not be sufficient. To supplement, evaporative cooling, shade cloth or paint are used.

Humidity levels are also important in greenhouses. Relative humidity should be around 70 to 85 percent, especially during high-growth periods. High humidity levels may cause early bolting and fungal diseases. One way of decreasing humidity levels is by venting or exhausting humid air and watering only when necessary. In dry climates, humidity levels can be increased in a greenhouse by spraying water on the floor.

In the spring and fall seasons when the weather is cool and moist, high humidity is more of a problem compared to the winter season. In freezing weather, high humidity is not possible because the relative humidity of the outside air is very low. Glass panes serve as natural dehumidifiers when the outside air is colder.

One function of a greenhouse is to provide a structure for crops that is transparent to sunlight, but adequately enclosed to diminish heat loss. Some of the solar radiation which goes through the covering produces heat, and some it is used for photosynthesis which results in the production of useful biomass.

Light intensity in a greenhouse is partially determined through its design. Fluorescent or LED lights can be used when growing spring seedlings, especially in cloudy regions. They are also very useful for midwinter greens and the last of the fall-fruiting crops. For sun-loving plants such as orchids and tomatoes, high-intensity discharge lighting systems can be set up. However, they are quite costly and they give off so much heat. Shading can also be used to screen out light especially during summer. Shade fabric panels can be used and there are options from light shade to heavy shade. They're attached to the greenhouse roof, and the part that has the most intense heat can be covered up. Shading paint that's specifically developed for greenhouses can also be used. This paint can be easily washed off before winter, when more light will be needed.

In order to have a proper working greenhouse, water supply is necessary. Hand watering is the simplest form of watering system, but if no one can regularly do the task, automatic watering systems are available. To control these watering systems, mechanical evaporation sensors or time clocks are used. There are a variety of automatic watering systems and they work in different ways. One method that is ideal for plants in pots is feeding water through a series of feed drips in a pipe. For plants growing directly from the earth, an ideal watering method would be spreading through a porous hose.

An alternative method in watering a greenhouse is the passive watering system. This uses capillary matting to get water from a reservoir, where it passes through a length of gutter that is installed over the edge of the greenhouse benches. As long the reservoir is full, the plants will be watered.

A properly managed greenhouse environment can yield a variety of crops, such as vegetables, fruits, herbs, and ornamental plants such as ferns, palms, cacti, orchids and flowers.

Chapter 13: Growing Vegetables in Greenhouses

Growing vegetables in a greenhouse is fulfilling because we can get produce all year round. We can grow either cool season vegetables or warm season vegetables in greenhouses.

For cool season vegetables, the ideal temperature within the greenhouse would be 50 degrees to 70 degrees Fahrenheit, while night time temperatures can range from 45 degrees to 55 degrees Fahrenheit.

Cool season vegetables tend to spoil or fail to pollinate in warm temperatures. Cold season vegetables that we can grow in a greenhouse are beets, carrots, broccoli, cabbage, cauliflower, chard, leaf lettuce, peas, radish, spinach and turnips.

Beets can be grown in the fall and held in the greenhouse during the winter months. Carrots needs adequate water and cooler temperatures to thrive, and they require 12 inch deep containers since they are root crops. Broccoli, cabbage and cauliflower have high yield for the space used, and we need to be careful because they tend to split their heads in warm humid conditions. Chard does very well inside a greenhouse, while leaf lettuce is easy to grow in the fall, winter or spring in a solar greenhouse. Peas do not transplant well, so it is not well suited for container gardening. Radishes are good for spring and fall in a greenhouse, but they need 12 hours of light in order to root. Best spinach quality comes from a greenhouse that has a cooler temperature, from 45 degrees to 50 degrees Fahrenheit. Also, it is sensitive to temperature fluctuations. Turnips are ideal for fall and spring.

Greenhouse Gardening for Beginners 2nd Edition

In growing warm season vegetables, high light intensity is needed with moderate temperatures at night. During the winter, they can be grown in a greenhouse using solar heat collectors. Greenhouse climate control systems are needed in winter for these crops to produce. These accessories make it a bit costly to grow warm season vegetables during winter time.

Temperature requirements of warm season crops in the daytime are 60 degrees to 85 degrees Fahrenheit. At night time, they need 55 degrees Fahrenheit to 65 degrees Fahrenheit.

Warm season vegetables that we can grow in a greenhouse are eggplants, beans, cucumbers, peppers, summer squash or zucchini, tomatoes, although tomatoes are classified as fruits and leafy vegetables.

In sowing eggplants, hand pollination is required. They need containers that are 8 inches deep. Beans are not common greenhouse crops, and they have poor winter production. However, they will yield good production with adequate light and good spacing in the spring and fall.

Cucumbers require high humidity, good moisture, good air circulation and high light intensity. They need about 75 degrees to 80 degrees Fahrenheit day time temperature and about 50 degrees night time temperature for pollen to develop.

There are many pepper varieties that can be grown in a greenhouse environment as well. Peppers also need a container size that is at least 8 inches deep. To enjoy the best crop of peppers, a warm environment, regular watering and a good drainage system are necessary.

Like eggplants, hand pollination is also required to sow summer squash or zucchini. Tomatoes need a container that's 12 inches deep with a minimum of 55 degrees Fahrenheit night temperature for pollen to grow. There a lot of varieties of leafy vegetables, such as spinach and lettuce that grow well in a greenhouse environment with temperature that is above 50 degrees Fahrenheit.

Chapter 14: Growing Fruits in Greenhouses

Aside from vegetables, fruits can also be grown in a greenhouse. There are certain places in the world where home fruit growing is limited due to climate or weather conditions. However, these natural conditions should not be a limitation with a greenhouse. In a greenhouse, fruit trees, shrubs and vines can be grown at any time of the year. A great diversity of fruit can be cultivated in a controlled or semi-controlled environment.

Growing fruit trees in the greenhouse needs a warm environment for them to thrive. The temperature should be above 50 degrees Fahrenheit, while tropical fruit trees require temperatures above 60 degrees Fahrenheit.

We will be discussing different kinds of fruits that can be grown in a greenhouse, along with some techniques and methods on how to grow them.

Grape vines can grow well in a greenhouse, with proper care and proper variety selection. Grape varieties that can thrive in a greenhouse setting are Buckland Sweetwater and Black Hamburgh. Planting should ideally be done in December when the vine is dormant. However, the plants are grown in a pot and can be planted any time of the year. The most crucial aspect of cultivation for vines is free-draining soil. It is important to get this right because water-logged soils can damage vines. The crops must be thoroughly watered to ensure that they reach the roots. The vine should be trained to grow up into the roof of the greenhouse. As the fruits develop, they need to be pruned to allow the grapes enough space to grow into a good size.

Strawberries are also grown in greenhouses in many parts of the world. In China, strawberries are grown over winter in greenhouses that rely on solar energy for heat. The temperature of strawberry cultivation should not rise above 16 degrees Celsius because this will hold back flowering. Pollination should be done by hand. When fruits start to develop, it is a good idea to insert straw underneath them in order to keep the fruits from rotting on the soil. You may also use fiber mats. The mats will help stifle weeds. If weeds do grow, you should pull them out by hand. Strawberries are very productive for three years, but they need to be replaced after that. Crop rotation minimizes the risk of an infestation by pests and the occurrence of diseases.

Peaches, apricots and nectarines can grow in cool greenhouses. These stone fruits can take up a lot of space, but they can be pruned. A little time and effort is needed to maintain these trees, but it yields great rewards in the end. The trees are pruned into a fan shape. This provides sufficient room for the fruits to develop and makes harvesting them easier. The plants do need help with pollination, especially since insects are usually absent in a well-maintained greenhouse. The usual way is to transfer pollen manually using a small brush. This has to be done every day throughout the flowering period.

A variety of citrus fruits such as lemons, grapefruit, tangerines and lemons can thrive in a greenhouse environment. They need a temperature of 55 degrees Fahrenheit for the seeds to germinate. The process from sowing the seed to the time the trees actually produce fruit may take up to ten years. When growers want to plant a tree that produces a favored fruit, they graft a budding branch to a dwarf rootstock. These varieties grow a bit larger than dwarf tress but are still smaller than the standard-sized citrus trees. The size has to be maintained with regular pruning because they will eventually grow too large for the greenhouse if not done so.

Melons are planted directly into the ground in a greenhouse or into six-inch deep pots, with the seed placed about half an inch deep. The ideal months for planting melons seeds would be from April to May. As soon as the seedlings appear, over-watering them is not recommended because it can cause the melons to split. As the plants increase in height, side shoots should be pruned out in order to direct growth on the main shoot. If the melons were started in pots, it would be better to replant them into a raised bed in the greenhouse, as this will give the plant more space to spread out. Provide support such as wires or wooden sticks as the melon plants grow to support their weight.

Chapter 15: Growing Herbs in Greenhouses

Generally, the processes in growing herbs are similar to growing vegetables. However, there are some practices specific to herb production. Growing greenhouse herbs has a lot to do with healthy soil. Temperatures also need to be adjusted to protect herbs from the cold. Fertility and irrigation also has to be managed a bit differently.

Basil is the easiest herb to grow in a greenhouse because it can be sown all year round. Perennials such as thyme and rosemary can be propagated in late winter. Since there is little natural light in the winter, fluorescent lights can be the source of light within. Marjoram, dill, parsley and cilantro can be sown as seeds in the greenhouse, and then moved out to cold frames in the spring. Fast growing herbs such as chives, basil and dill become overgrown if started too early. Different varieties of mint are ideal for greenhouse growing. Since it is an invasive plant, it is recommended that they are planted in a container. 100 degrees Fahrenheit is the proper temperature for herbs.

Herbs thrive and flourish when they are dried out well between watering. Too much watering may cause the slow growth or diminished oil content, which means the herb's aroma or culinary content is diminished. Even though they love heat, we have to watch for overheating. Shade and ventilation is needed, and greenhouses with diffused light are recommended for herbs. Herbs can help control pests. Parsley, fennel, rosemary and dill attract wasps that destroy aphids.

Chapter 16: Growing Ornamental Plants in a Greenhouse

A wide variety of ornamentals can be grown inside a greenhouse. In fact some of these plants thrive better in the protected environment versus an open garden. Ornamental plants may be classified into either sun-loving or shade-loving annuals or perennials, and may even be further grouped according to their distinct features or particular needs. Ferns, palms and tropical plants such as cacti and orchids can be grown inside a greenhouse.

Ferns thrive in the greenhouse if the climate is controlled accordingly. Since ferns thrive in tropical and sub-tropical environments, humidity must be set to a higher level. Ferns love moisture in the air, so the use of a humidifier is recommended. To do this the trays on which the pots are standing should be on a bed of damp pebbles. Ferns also need to be regularly misted with water. The right compost for ferns should be free draining so that their roots do not get waterlogged. Since ferns are forest or woodland plants, they need to have soil that is never allowed to dry out. This means that they need to be watered every day. The light level should be in a place where the ferns get the most out of the morning or late afternoon sun, but direct sunlight will make them lose their leaves or discolor the leaves. Ferns can also be placed in dim light, and then regularly placed under bright artificial light, such as a fluorescent strip or a special gardening bulb. Most ferns thrive in a temperature ranging from 60 degrees to 70 degrees Fahrenheit.

Palms are adaptable plants and can also be grown inside a greenhouse. They can handle winter temperature not less than 50 degrees Fahrenheit. They prefer glazed lighting, and under direct sunlight the leaves can turn yellow or bleached out. Shade cloths can be used on plastic greenhouses. However, one should also balance the light intensity because too little light produces green but stretched out and unstable plants. Mounting palms on benches makes them avoid colder ground temperature and gives them more air circulation. Since they grow faster in the greenhouse, dead leaves have to be regularly pruned.

Tropical plants such as cacti and orchids have a place in the right greenhouse. Cacti need a lot of light and a dry surface. These plants can occupy the sunniest spots in the greenhouse. Most cacti and other succulents remain drier in the cooler months. They are prone to over-watering, so allow the soil to dry before watering again.

Orchids also thrive in a greenhouse environment as long as the right temperature is provided. Different types of orchids grow at different temperatures. You need to stick to one temperature region. The temperature range for cool climate orchids are 45 degrees Fahrenheit for winter night temperatures to 57 degrees Fahrenheit for a maximum summer night temperature. A warm climate orchid should have a minimum night temperature of 57 degrees Fahrenheit and a maximum night temperate of 72 degrees Fahrenheit. The greenhouse temperature should be maintained in order for the orchids to thrive. If you wish to grow orchids from different climate zones, dividing greenhouse into different temperature levels will do the trick, but strict monitoring is needed for that. Orchids should not be subjected to direct heat, so shade cloths are necessary during hotter weather.

A variety of orchid called phalanenopsis is native to India, Indonesia and the Philippines. If you want to propagate these orchids, you have to match the temperature in these countries. The greenhouse would then require very bright light. They need to be grown at a temperature that does not exceed 85 degrees Fahrenheit during day time or go below 55 degrees Fahrenheit at night.

Orchids such as cynmbidium and dendrobium work best at warmer temperatures but can also handle cooler temperatures. They need as much light as possible but not direct sunlight.

Flowers grow well in a greenhouse environment and can be raised from seeds. The advantage of growing flowers in a greenhouse is that it extends the productive season of the plants. Petunias, geraniums, Amazon lily, and African violet can thrive in a greenhouse environment as long as temperature is monitored and moderate light conditions are followed.

Conclusion

Thank you again for purchasing this book!

I hope this book was able to help you to do gardening inside a greenhouse.

The next step is to use the tips mentioned here to create the plantation of your dreams while doing it indoors.

Finally, if you enjoyed this book, please take the time to share your thoughts and post a review on Amazon. We do our best to reach out to readers and provide the best value we can. Your positive review will help us achieve that. It'd be greatly appreciated!

Thank you and good luck!

Check Out My Other Books

Below you'll find some of my other popular books that are popular on Amazon and Kindle as well. Simply click on the links below to check them out. Alternatively, you can visit my author page on Amazon to see other work done by me.

Coconut Oil for Skin Care & Hair Loss

http://amzn.to/1poGwGC

Coconut Oil & Weight Loss for Beginners

http://amzn.to/1jqdy3R

Walk Your Way To Weight Loss

http://amzn.to/1jOHpgy

Quick Easy Healthy Snack Ideas for Kids

http://amzn.to/1grvURn

Oil Pulling for Beginners

http://amzn.to/SBDoXb

Healing Babies & Children With Aromatherapy For Beginners

http://amzn.to/TOHJHs

Carb Cycling for Fast Easy Weight Loss
http://amzn.to/THn8Vl

Beauty Products for Beginners
http://amzn.to/1nVvwNw

Body Lotions for Beginners
http://amzn.to/S3XlWh

Container Gardening for Beginners
http://amzn.to/1oLb2po

Vegetable Gardening for beginners
http://amzn.to/1lqCCIK

Raised Bed Gardening for beginners
http://amzn.to/1nHY0ry

Companion Gardening for beginners
http://amzn.to/1hYzeEl

Greenhouse Gardening for Beginners 2nd Edition

Essential Oils Box Set #1 Healing Babies and Children With Aromatherapy for Beginners & Oil Pulling for Beginners

http://amzn.to/1yZoH0Q

Essential Oils Box Set #2 Carb Cycling For Fast Easy Weight Loss + Walk Your Way to Weight Loss

http://amzn.to/Tu5xiL

Essential Oils Box Set #3 Beauty Products For Beginners + Body Lotions For Beginners

http://amzn.to/1qnVLNQ

Essential Oils Box Set #4 Coconut Oil & Weigh Loss for Beginners & Coconut Oil for Skin Care & Hair Loss

http://amzn.to/1iQQUlN

Essential Oils Box Set #5 Coconut Oil Skin Care & Hair Loss + Healing Babies & Children & Aromatherapy for Beginners + Beauty Products for Beginners +Body Lotions For Beginners +Oil Pulling for Beginners

http://amzn.to/1qGPc6D

Essential Oils Box Set #6Carb Cycling for Fast Easy Weight Loss + Oil Pulling Therapy For Beginners + Walk Your Way to Weight Loss + Coconut Oil & Weight for Beginners + Coconut Oil for Skin Care & Hair Loss

Greenhouse Gardening for Beginners 2nd Edition

http://amzn.to/UXAAoz

Essential Oils Box Set #7 Coconut Oil for Skin Care & Hair Loss + Oil Pulling Therapy For Beginners + Healing Babies and Children with Aromatherapy for Beginners

http://amzn.to/1nUdbg5

Gardening Box Set #1 Raised Bed Gardening For Beginners + Vegetable Gardening For Beginners + Companion Gardening For Beginners + Greenhouse Gardening for Beginners +Container Gardening for Beginners

http://amzn.to/1lZOsse

Gardening Box Set #2 Container Gardening For Beginners + Ultimate Guide to Companion Gardening for Beginners

http://amzn.to/1q4wma5

If the links do not work, for whatever reason, you can simply search for these titles on the Amazon website to find them.

12148 Hillman Dr
Palm Beach Gardens
FL 33410

Made in the USA
Middletown, DE
05 November 2015